ISBN 979-8-9878563-6-9

US $ 14.99

51499 >

Morning Gratefulness

Date: _____

Today I want to feel...

_____
_____
_____

Today I will spread kindness by...

_____
_____
_____

3 things I'm grateful for today are...

_____
_____
_____

"Happiness is a habit."

Today I'm thankful for...

Date: _____

Evening Gratefulness

3 things I'm grateful for today are...

_____
_____
_____

The best part of today was...

_____
_____
_____

What can I learn from today's experiences?

_____
_____
_____

Tomorrow I'm looking forward to...

_____
_____
_____

"Do more of what you love."

Things I'm proud of achieving today are...

_____

_____

_____

_____

_____

_____

_____

_____

_____

_____

_____

_____

_____

_____

_____

_____

"Believe. You're halfway there."

Mental health check in

DATE _____

HOW ARE YOU FEELING TODAY?

HOW ARE YOU FEELING TODAY?

HOW CAN YOU IMPROVE YOUR MENTAL HEALTH?

WHAT HAVE BEEN YOUR THREE DOMINANT EMOTIONS THIS WEEK?

○ _____

○ _____

○ _____

WHAT DO YOU FEEL GOOD ABOUT RIGHT NOW?

THINGS THAT TRIGGERS NEGATIVE EMOTIONS

○ _____

○ _____

○ _____

○ _____

MY RANKING OF MY MENTAL HEALTH THIS WEEK

☆ ☆ ☆ ☆ ☆

Morning Gratefulness

Date: _____

Today I want to feel...

_____

_____

_____

Today I will spread kindness by...

_____

_____

_____

3 things I'm grateful for today are...

_____

_____

_____

"Happiness is a habit."

Today I'm thankful for...

Date: _____

Evening Gratefulness

3 things I'm grateful for today are...

_____

_____

_____

The best part of today was...

_____

_____

_____

What can I learn from today's experiences?

_____

_____

_____

Tomorrow I'm looking forward to...

_____

_____

_____

"Do more of what you love."

Things I'm proud of achieving today are...

_____

_____

_____

_____

_____

_____

_____

_____

_____

_____

_____

_____

_____

_____

_____

_____

_____

"Believe. You're halfway there."

Mental health check in

DATE _____

HOW ARE YOU FEELING TODAY?

HOW ARE YOU FEELING TODAY?

HOW CAN YOU IMPROVE YOUR
MENTAL HEALTH?

WHAT HAVE BEEN YOUR THREE
DOMINANT EMOTIONS THIS WEEK?

○ _____

○ _____

○ _____

WHAT DO YOU FEEL GOOD ABOUT
RIGHT NOW?

THINGS THAT TRIGGERS NEGATIVE
EMOTIONS

○ _____

○ _____

○ _____

○ _____

MY RANKING OF MY MENTAL
HEALTH THIS WEEK

☆ ☆ ☆ ☆ ☆

Morning Gratefulness

Date: _____

Today I want to feel...

_____
_____
_____

Today I will spread kindness by...

_____
_____
_____

3 things I'm grateful for today are...

_____
_____
_____

"Happiness is a habit."

Today I'm thankful for...

Date: _____

Evening Gratefulness

3 things I'm grateful for today are...

_____

_____

_____

The best part of today was...

_____

_____

_____

What can I learn from today's experiences?

_____

_____

_____

Tomorrow I'm looking forward to...

_____

_____

_____

"Do more of what you love."

Things I'm proud of achieving today are...

_____

_____

_____

_____

_____

_____

_____

_____

_____

_____

_____

_____

_____

_____

_____

_____

"Believe. You're halfway there."

Mental health check in

DATE _____

HOW ARE YOU FEELING TODAY?

HOW ARE YOU FEELING TODAY?

HOW CAN YOU IMPROVE YOUR MENTAL HEALTH?

WHAT HAVE BEEN YOUR THREE DOMINANT EMOTIONS THIS WEEK?

○ _____

○ _____

○ _____

WHAT DO YOU FEEL GOOD ABOUT RIGHT NOW?

THINGS THAT TRIGGERS NEGATIVE EMOTIONS

○ _____

○ _____

○ _____

○ _____

MY RANKING OF MY MENTAL HEALTH THIS WEEK

☆ ☆ ☆ ☆ ☆

Morning Gratefulness

Date: _____

Today I want to feel...

_____

_____

_____

Today I will spread kindness by...

_____

_____

_____

3 things I'm grateful for today are...

_____

_____

_____

"Happiness is a habit."

Today I'm thankful for...

Date: _____

Evening Gratefulness

3 things I'm grateful for today are...

_____

_____

_____

The best part of today was...

_____

_____

_____

What can I learn from today's experiences?

_____

_____

_____

Tomorrow I'm looking forward to...

_____

_____

_____

"Do more of what you love."

Things I'm proud of achieving today are...

_____

_____

_____

_____

_____

_____

_____

_____

_____

_____

_____

_____

_____

_____

"Believe. You're halfway there."

Mental health check in

DATE _____

HOW ARE YOU FEELING TODAY?

WHAT HAVE BEEN YOUR THREE DOMINANT EMOTIONS THIS WEEK?

○ _____

○ _____

○ _____

WHAT DO YOU FEEL GOOD ABOUT RIGHT NOW?

HOW ARE YOU FEELING TODAY?

HOW CAN YOU IMPROVE YOUR MENTAL HEALTH?

THINGS THAT TRIGGERS NEGATIVE EMOTIONS

○ _____

○ _____

○ _____

○ _____

MY RANKING OF MY MENTAL HEALTH THIS WEEK

☆ ☆ ☆ ☆ ☆

Morning Gratefulness

Date: _____

Today I want to feel...

_____
_____
_____

Today I will spread kindness by...

_____
_____
_____

3 things I'm grateful for today are...

_____
_____
_____

"Happiness is a habit."

Today I'm thankful for...

Date: _____

Evening Gratefulness

3 things I'm grateful for today are...

_____

_____

_____

The best part of today was...

_____

_____

_____

What can I learn from today's experiences?

_____

_____

_____

Tomorrow I'm looking forward to...

_____

_____

_____

"Do more of what you love."

Things I'm proud of achieving today are...

_____

_____

_____

_____

_____

_____

_____

_____

_____

_____

_____

_____

_____

_____

_____

_____

"Believe. You're halfway there."

Mental health check in

DATE _____

HOW ARE YOU FEELING TODAY?

HOW ARE YOU FEELING TODAY?

HOW CAN YOU IMPROVE YOUR
MENTAL HEALTH?

WHAT HAVE BEEN YOUR THREE
DOMINANT EMOTIONS THIS WEEK?

○ _____

○ _____

○ _____

WHAT DO YOU FEEL GOOD ABOUT
RIGHT NOW?

THINGS THAT TRIGGERS NEGATIVE
EMOTIONS

○ _____

○ _____

○ _____

○ _____

MY RANKING OF MY MENTAL
HEALTH THIS WEEK

☆ ☆ ☆ ☆ ☆

Morning Gratefulness

Date: _____

Today I want to feel...

_____

_____

_____

Today I will spread kindness by...

_____

_____

_____

3 things I'm grateful for today are...

_____

_____

_____

"Happiness is a habit."

Today I'm thankful for...

Date: _____

Evening Gratefulness

3 things I'm grateful for today are...

_____

_____

_____

The best part of today was...

_____

_____

_____

What can I learn from today's experiences?

_____

_____

_____

Tomorrow I'm looking forward to...

_____

_____

_____

"Do more of what you love."

Things I'm proud of achieving today are...

_____

_____

_____

_____

_____

_____

_____

_____

_____

_____

_____

_____

_____

_____

_____

_____

_____

"Believe. You're halfway there."

Mental health check in

DATE _____

HOW ARE YOU FEELING TODAY?

HOW ARE YOU FEELING TODAY?

HOW CAN YOU IMPROVE YOUR MENTAL HEALTH?

WHAT HAVE BEEN YOUR THREE DOMINANT EMOTIONS THIS WEEK?

○ _____

○ _____

○ _____

WHAT DO YOU FEEL GOOD ABOUT RIGHT NOW?

THINGS THAT TRIGGERS NEGATIVE EMOTIONS

○ _____

○ _____

○ _____

○ _____

MY RANKING OF MY MENTAL HEALTH THIS WEEK

☆ ☆ ☆ ☆ ☆

Morning Gratefulness

Date: _____

Today I want to feel...

_____

_____

_____

Today I will spread kindness by...

_____

_____

_____

3 things I'm grateful for today are...

_____

_____

_____

"Happiness is a habit."

Today I'm thankful for...

Date: _____

Evening Gratefulness

3 things I'm grateful for today are...

_____

_____

_____

The best part of today was...

_____

_____

_____

What can I learn from today's experiences?

_____

_____

_____

Tomorrow I'm looking forward to...

_____

_____

_____

"Do more of what you love."

Things I'm proud of achieving today are...

_____

_____

_____

_____

_____

_____

_____

_____

_____

_____

_____

_____

_____

_____

_____

_____

"Believe. You're halfway there."

Mental health check in

DATE _____

HOW ARE YOU FEELING TODAY?

HOW ARE YOU FEELING TODAY?

HOW CAN YOU IMPROVE YOUR MENTAL HEALTH?

WHAT HAVE BEEN YOUR THREE DOMINANT EMOTIONS THIS WEEK?

○ _____

○ _____

○ _____

WHAT DO YOU FEEL GOOD ABOUT RIGHT NOW?

THINGS THAT TRIGGERS NEGATIVE EMOTIONS

○ _____

○ _____

○ _____

○ _____

MY RANKING OF MY MENTAL HEALTH THIS WEEK

☆ ☆ ☆ ☆ ☆

Morning Gratefulness

Date: _____

Today I want to feel...

_____

_____

_____

Today I will spread kindness by...

_____

_____

_____

3 things I'm grateful for today are...

_____

_____

_____

"Happiness is a habit."

Today I'm thankful for...

Date: _____

Evening Gratefulness

3 things I'm grateful for today are...

_____

_____

_____

The best part of today was...

_____

_____

_____

What can I learn from today's experiences?

_____

_____

_____

Tomorrow I'm looking forward to...

_____

_____

_____

"Do more of what you love."

Things I'm proud of achieving today are...

_____
_____
_____
_____
_____
_____
_____
_____
_____
_____
_____
_____
_____
_____
_____
_____
_____

"Believe. You're halfway there."

Mental health check in

DATE _____

HOW ARE YOU FEELING TODAY?

HOW ARE YOU FEELING TODAY?

HOW CAN YOU IMPROVE YOUR MENTAL HEALTH?

WHAT HAVE BEEN YOUR THREE DOMINANT EMOTIONS THIS WEEK?

○ _____
○ _____
○ _____

WHAT DO YOU FEEL GOOD ABOUT RIGHT NOW?

THINGS THAT TRIGGERS NEGATIVE EMOTIONS

○ _____
○ _____
○ _____
○ _____

MY RANKING OF MY MENTAL HEALTH THIS WEEK

☆ ☆ ☆ ☆ ☆

Morning Gratefulness

Date: _____

Today I want to feel...

_____
_____
_____

Today I will spread kindness by...

_____
_____
_____

3 things I'm grateful for today are...

_____
_____
_____

"Happiness is a habit."

Today I'm thankful for...

Date: _____

Evening Gratefulness

3 things I'm grateful for today are...

_____

_____

_____

The best part of today was...

_____

_____

_____

What can I learn from today's experiences?

_____

_____

_____

Tomorrow I'm looking forward to...

_____

_____

_____

"Do more of what you love."

Things I'm proud of achieving today are...

_____

_____

_____

_____

_____

_____

_____

_____

_____

_____

_____

_____

_____

_____

_____

_____

"Believe. You're halfway there."

Mental health check in

DATE _____

HOW ARE YOU FEELING TODAY?

HOW ARE YOU FEELING TODAY?

HOW CAN YOU IMPROVE YOUR MENTAL HEALTH?

WHAT HAVE BEEN YOUR THREE DOMINANT EMOTIONS THIS WEEK?

○ _____

○ _____

○ _____

WHAT DO YOU FEEL GOOD ABOUT RIGHT NOW?

THINGS THAT TRIGGERS NEGATIVE EMOTIONS

○ _____

○ _____

○ _____

○ _____

MY RANKING OF MY MENTAL HEALTH THIS WEEK

☆ ☆ ☆ ☆ ☆

Morning Gratefulness

Date: _____

Today I want to feel...

_____

_____

_____

Today I will spread kindness by...

_____

_____

_____

3 things I'm grateful for today are...

_____

_____

_____

"Happiness is a habit."

Today I'm thankful for...

Date: _____

Evening Gratefulness

3 things I'm grateful for today are...

_____

_____

_____

The best part of today was...

_____

_____

_____

What can I learn from today's experiences?

_____

_____

_____

Tomorrow I'm looking forward to...

_____

_____

_____

"Do more of what you love."

Things I'm proud of achieving today are...

_____
_____
_____
_____
_____
_____
_____
_____
_____
_____
_____
_____
_____
_____
_____
_____
_____

"Believe. You're halfway there."

Mental health check in

DATE _____

HOW ARE YOU FEELING TODAY?

HOW ARE YOU FEELING TODAY?

HOW CAN YOU IMPROVE YOUR MENTAL HEALTH?

WHAT HAVE BEEN YOUR THREE DOMINANT EMOTIONS THIS WEEK?

○ _____

○ _____

○ _____

WHAT DO YOU FEEL GOOD ABOUT RIGHT NOW?

THINGS THAT TRIGGERS NEGATIVE EMOTIONS

○ _____

○ _____

○ _____

○ _____

MY RANKING OF MY MENTAL HEALTH THIS WEEK

☆ ☆ ☆ ☆ ☆

Morning Gratefulness

Date: _____

Today I want to feel...

_____

_____

_____

Today I will spread kindness by...

_____

_____

_____

3 things I'm grateful for today are...

_____

_____

_____

"Happiness is a habit."

Today I'm thankful for...

Date: _____

Evening Gratefulness

3 things I'm grateful for today are...

_____

_____

_____

The best part of today was...

_____

_____

_____

What can I learn from today's experiences?

_____

_____

_____

Tomorrow I'm looking forward to...

_____

_____

_____

"Do more of what you love."

Things I'm proud of achieving today are...

_____

_____

_____

_____

_____

_____

_____

_____

_____

_____

_____

_____

_____

_____

_____

_____

_____

"Believe. You're halfway there."

Mental health check in

DATE _____

HOW ARE YOU FEELING TODAY?

HOW ARE YOU FEELING TODAY?

HOW CAN YOU IMPROVE YOUR
MENTAL HEALTH?

WHAT HAVE BEEN YOUR THREE
DOMINANT EMOTIONS THIS WEEK?

○ _____

○ _____

○ _____

WHAT DO YOU FEEL GOOD ABOUT
RIGHT NOW?

THINGS THAT TRIGGERS NEGATIVE
EMOTIONS

○ _____

○ _____

○ _____

○ _____

MY RANKING OF MY MENTAL
HEALTH THIS WEEK

☆ ☆ ☆ ☆ ☆

Morning Gratefulness

Date: _____

Today I want to feel...

_____
_____
_____

Today I will spread kindness by...

_____
_____
_____

3 things I'm grateful for today are...

_____
_____
_____

"Happiness is a habit."

Today I'm thankful for...

Date: _____

Evening Gratefulness

3 things I'm grateful for today are...

_____

_____

_____

The best part of today was...

_____

_____

_____

What can I learn from today's experiences?

_____

_____

_____

Tomorrow I'm looking forward to...

_____

_____

_____

"Do more of what you love."

Things I'm proud of achieving today are...

_____

_____

_____

_____

_____

_____

_____

_____

_____

_____

_____

_____

_____

_____

_____

_____

_____

"Believe. You're halfway there."

Mental health check in

DATE _____

HOW ARE YOU FEELING TODAY?

HOW ARE YOU FEELING TODAY?

HOW CAN YOU IMPROVE YOUR
MENTAL HEALTH?

WHAT HAVE BEEN YOUR THREE
DOMINANT EMOTIONS THIS WEEK?

○ _____
○ _____
○ _____

WHAT DO YOU FEEL GOOD ABOUT
RIGHT NOW?

THINGS THAT TRIGGERS NEGATIVE
EMOTIONS

○ _____
○ _____
○ _____
○ _____

MY RANKING OF MY MENTAL
HEALTH THIS WEEK

☆ ☆ ☆ ☆ ☆

Morning Gratefulness

Date: _____

Today I want to feel...

_____
_____
_____

Today I will spread kindness by...

_____
_____
_____

3 things I'm grateful for today are...

_____
_____
_____

"Happiness is a habit."

Today I'm thankful for...

Date: _____

Evening Gratefulness

3 things I'm grateful for today are...

_____

_____

_____

The best part of today was...

_____

_____

_____

What can I learn from today's experiences?

_____

_____

_____

Tomorrow I'm looking forward to...

_____

_____

_____

"Do more of what you love."

Things I'm proud of achieving today are...

_____
_____
_____
_____
_____
_____
_____
_____
_____
_____
_____
_____
_____
_____
_____
_____

"Believe. You're halfway there."

Mental health check in

DATE _____

HOW ARE YOU FEELING TODAY?

WHAT HAVE BEEN YOUR THREE DOMINANT EMOTIONS THIS WEEK?

○ _____

○ _____

○ _____

WHAT DO YOU FEEL GOOD ABOUT RIGHT NOW?

HOW ARE YOU FEELING TODAY?

HOW CAN YOU IMPROVE YOUR MENTAL HEALTH?

THINGS THAT TRIGGERS NEGATIVE EMOTIONS

○ _____

○ _____

○ _____

○ _____

MY RANKING OF MY MENTAL HEALTH THIS WEEK

☆ ☆ ☆ ☆ ☆

Morning Gratefulness

Date: _____

Today I want to feel...

_____

_____

_____

Today I will spread kindness by...

_____

_____

_____

3 things I'm grateful for today are...

_____

_____

_____

"Happiness is a habit."

Today I'm thankful for...   Date: _____

_____
_____
_____
_____
_____
_____
_____
_____
_____
_____
_____
_____
_____
_____
_____
_____
_____
_____
_____
_____
_____
_____
_____

Evening Gratefulness

3 things I'm grateful for today are...

_____

_____

_____

The best part of today was...

_____

_____

_____

What can I learn from today's experiences?

_____

_____

_____

Tomorrow I'm looking forward to...

_____

_____

_____

"Do more of what you love."

Things I'm proud of achieving today are...

_____

_____

_____

_____

_____

_____

_____

_____

_____

_____

_____

_____

_____

_____

_____

_____

_____

"Believe. You're halfway there."

Mental health check in

DATE _____

HOW ARE YOU FEELING TODAY?

HOW ARE YOU FEELING TODAY?

HOW CAN YOU IMPROVE YOUR
MENTAL HEALTH?

WHAT HAVE BEEN YOUR THREE
DOMINANT EMOTIONS THIS WEEK?

○ _____

○ _____

○ _____

WHAT DO YOU FEEL GOOD ABOUT
RIGHT NOW?

THINGS THAT TRIGGERS NEGATIVE
EMOTIONS

○ _____

○ _____

○ _____

○ _____

MY RANKING OF MY MENTAL
HEALTH THIS WEEK

☆ ☆ ☆ ☆ ☆

Morning Gratefulness

Date: _____

Today I want to feel...

_____

_____

_____

Today I will spread kindness by...

_____

_____

_____

3 things I'm grateful for today are...

_____

_____

_____

"Happiness is a habit."

Today I'm thankful for...

Date: _____

Evening Gratefulness

3 things I'm grateful for today are...

_____
_____
_____

The best part of today was...

_____
_____
_____

What can I learn from today's experiences?

_____
_____

Tomorrow I'm looking forward to...

_____
_____
_____

"Do more of what you love."

Things I'm proud of achieving today are...

_____

_____

_____

_____

_____

_____

_____

_____

_____

_____

_____

_____

_____

_____

_____

_____

"Believe. You're halfway there."

Mental health check in

DATE _____

HOW ARE YOU FEELING TODAY?

HOW ARE YOU FEELING TODAY?

HOW CAN YOU IMPROVE YOUR
MENTAL HEALTH?

WHAT HAVE BEEN YOUR THREE
DOMINANT EMOTIONS THIS WEEK?

○ _____

○ _____

○ _____

WHAT DO YOU FEEL GOOD ABOUT
RIGHT NOW?

THINGS THAT TRIGGERS NEGATIVE
EMOTIONS

○ _____

○ _____

○ _____

○ _____

MY RANKING OF MY MENTAL
HEALTH THIS WEEK

☆ ☆ ☆ ☆ ☆

Morning Gratefulness

Date: _____

Today I want to feel...

_____

_____

_____

Today I will spread kindness by...

_____

_____

_____

3 things I'm grateful for today are...

_____

_____

_____

"Happiness is a habit."

Today I'm thankful for...

Date: _____

Evening Gratefulness

3 things I'm grateful for today are...

_____

_____

_____

The best part of today was...

_____

_____

_____

What can I learn from today's experiences?

_____

_____

_____

Tomorrow I'm looking forward to...

_____

_____

_____

"Do more of what you love."

Things I'm proud of achieving today are...

_____
_____
_____
_____
_____
_____
_____
_____
_____
_____
_____
_____
_____
_____
_____
_____
_____

"Believe. You're halfway there."

Mental health check in

DATE _____

HOW ARE YOU FEELING TODAY?

HOW ARE YOU FEELING TODAY?

HOW CAN YOU IMPROVE YOUR
MENTAL HEALTH?

WHAT HAVE BEEN YOUR THREE
DOMINANT EMOTIONS THIS WEEK?

○ _____
○ _____
○ _____

WHAT DO YOU FEEL GOOD ABOUT
RIGHT NOW?

THINGS THAT TRIGGERS NEGATIVE
EMOTIONS

○ _____
○ _____
○ _____
○ _____

MY RANKING OF MY MENTAL
HEALTH THIS WEEK

☆ ☆ ☆ ☆ ☆

Morning Gratefulness

Date: _____

Today I want to feel...

_____

_____

_____

Today I will spread kindness by...

_____

_____

_____

3 things I'm grateful for today are...

_____

_____

_____

"Happiness is a habit."

Today I'm thankful for...

Date: _____

Evening Gratefulness

3 things I'm grateful for today are...

_____

_____

_____

The best part of today was...

_____

_____

_____

What can I learn from today's experiences?

_____

_____

_____

Tomorrow I'm looking forward to...

_____

_____

_____

"Do more of what you love."

Things I'm proud of achieving today are...

_____

_____

_____

_____

_____

_____

_____

_____

_____

_____

_____

_____

_____

_____

_____

_____

_____

_____

"Believe. You're halfway there."

Mental health check in

DATE _____

HOW ARE YOU FEELING TODAY?

HOW ARE YOU FEELING TODAY?

HOW CAN YOU IMPROVE YOUR
MENTAL HEALTH?

WHAT HAVE BEEN YOUR THREE
DOMINANT EMOTIONS THIS WEEK?

○ _____

○ _____

○ _____

WHAT DO YOU FEEL GOOD ABOUT
RIGHT NOW?

THINGS THAT TRIGGERS NEGATIVE
EMOTIONS

○ _____

○ _____

○ _____

○ _____

MY RANKING OF MY MENTAL
HEALTH THIS WEEK

☆ ☆ ☆ ☆ ☆

Morning Gratefulness

Date: _____

Today I want to feel...

_____
_____
_____

Today I will spread kindness by...

_____
_____
_____

3 things I'm grateful for today are...

_____
_____
_____

"Happiness is a habit."

Today I'm thankful for...

Date: _____

_____
_____
_____
_____
_____
_____
_____
_____
_____
_____
_____
_____
_____
_____
_____
_____
_____
_____
_____
_____
_____
_____
_____
_____

Evening Gratefulness

3 things I'm grateful for today are...

_____

_____

_____

The best part of today was...

_____

_____

_____

What can I learn from today's experiences?

_____

_____

_____

Tomorrow I'm looking forward to...

_____

_____

_____

"Do more of what you love."

Things I'm proud of achieving today are...

_____
_____
_____
_____
_____
_____
_____
_____
_____
_____
_____
_____
_____
_____
_____
_____
_____

"Believe. You're halfway there."

Mental health check in

DATE _____

HOW ARE YOU FEELING TODAY?

_____

HOW ARE YOU FEELING TODAY?

HOW CAN YOU IMPROVE YOUR
MENTAL HEALTH?

WHAT HAVE BEEN YOUR THREE
DOMINANT EMOTIONS THIS WEEK?

○ _____
○ _____
○ _____

WHAT DO YOU FEEL GOOD ABOUT
RIGHT NOW?

THINGS THAT TRIGGERS NEGATIVE
EMOTIONS

○ _____
○ _____
○ _____
○ _____

MY RANKING OF MY MENTAL
HEALTH THIS WEEK

☆ ☆ ☆ ☆ ☆

Morning Gratefulness

Date: _____

Today I want to feel...

_____

_____

_____

Today I will spread kindness by...

_____

_____

_____

3 things I'm grateful for today are...

_____

_____

_____

"Happiness is a habit."

Today I'm thankful for...

Date: _____

Evening Gratefulness

3 things I'm grateful for today are...

_____

_____

_____

The best part of today was...

_____

_____

_____

What can I learn from today's experiences?

_____

_____

_____

Tomorrow I'm looking forward to...

_____

_____

_____

"Do more of what you love."

Things I'm proud of achieving today are...

_____
_____
_____
_____
_____
_____
_____
_____
_____
_____
_____
_____
_____
_____
_____
_____

"Believe. You're halfway there."

Mental health check in

DATE _____

HOW ARE YOU FEELING TODAY?

HOW ARE YOU FEELING TODAY?

HOW CAN YOU IMPROVE YOUR
MENTAL HEALTH?

WHAT HAVE BEEN YOUR THREE
DOMINANT EMOTIONS THIS WEEK?

○ _____

○ _____

○ _____

WHAT DO YOU FEEL GOOD ABOUT
RIGHT NOW?

THINGS THAT TRIGGERS NEGATIVE
EMOTIONS

○ _____

○ _____

○ _____

○ _____

MY RANKING OF MY MENTAL
HEALTH THIS WEEK

☆ ☆ ☆ ☆ ☆

Morning Gratefulness

Date: _____

Today I want to feel...

_____

_____

_____

Today I will spread kindness by...

_____

_____

_____

3 things I'm grateful for today are...

_____

_____

_____

"Happiness is a habit."

Today I'm thankful for...

Date: _____

Evening Gratefulness

3 things I'm grateful for today are...

_____

_____

_____

The best part of today was...

_____

_____

_____

What can I learn from today's experiences?

_____

_____

_____

Tomorrow I'm looking forward to...

_____

_____

_____

"Do more of what you love."

Things I'm proud of achieving today are...

_____

_____

_____

_____

_____

_____

_____

_____

_____

_____

_____

_____

_____

_____

_____

_____

_____

"Believe. You're halfway there."

Mental health check in

DATE _____

HOW ARE YOU FEELING TODAY?

HOW ARE YOU FEELING TODAY?

HOW CAN YOU IMPROVE YOUR MENTAL HEALTH?

WHAT HAVE BEEN YOUR THREE DOMINANT EMOTIONS THIS WEEK?

○ _____

○ _____

○ _____

WHAT DO YOU FEEL GOOD ABOUT RIGHT NOW?

THINGS THAT TRIGGERS NEGATIVE EMOTIONS

○ _____

○ _____

○ _____

○ _____

MY RANKING OF MY MENTAL HEALTH THIS WEEK

☆ ☆ ☆ ☆ ☆

www.ingramcontent.com/pod-product-compliance
Lightning Source LLC
Chambersburg PA
CBHW081133090426
42737CB00018B/3331